What Does a Firefighter Do?

by Susan Ring

Consultant: Mark Edelbrock, Firefighter, Seattle Fire Department

A firefighter's day is busy.
There are so many things to do.

Firefighters check the truck.

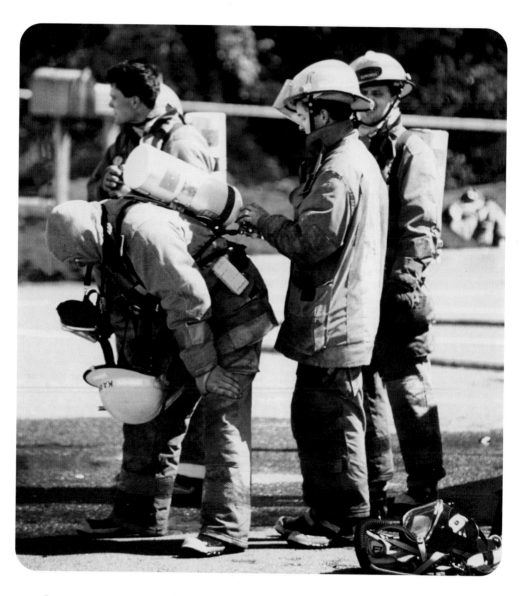

They check the other tools, too.

Firefighters rush into action
when the alarm rings.

Sometimes firefighters
use tools to get to a fire.

They spray the fire with plenty of water.

Firefighters use helicopters to fight forest fires.

They also dig around the fire to stop it from spreading.

Firefighters help when cars crash.

Firefighters also help people who are sick or hurt.

They carry the people to safety.

Firefighters help in other ways, too. They teach children about fighting fires.

They tell children what to do in case of a fire.

Firefighters also learn about new ways to fight fires. They practice what they have learned.

A firefighter's day is very busy.
Thank you, firefighters, for all
you do!